MW01181212

DATE DUE

Ray Bradbury

Titles in the *Authors Teens Love* series:

J.R.R. Tolkien
Master of Imaginary Worlds
0-7660-2246-3

Joan Lowery Nixon
Masterful Mystery Writer
0-7660-2194-7

Ray Bradbury
Master of Science Fiction and Fantasy
0-7660-2240-4

AUTHORS TEENS LOVE

Ray Bradbury

Master of Science Fiction and Fantasy

Wendy Mass

Enslow Publishers, Inc.

40 Industrial Road	PO Box 38
Box 398	Aldershot
Berkeley Heights, NJ 07922	Hants GU12 6BP
USA	UK

http://www.enslow.com

Library of Congress Cataloging-in-Publication Data

Mass, Wendy, 1967–
Ray Bradbury : master of science fiction and fantasy / Wendy Mass.
    v. cm. — (Authors teens love)
Includes bibliographical references and index.
Contents: Meeting the magicians—The wonder years—Hooray for
Hollywood—Bradbury's early career and marriage—The Martian
chronicles—Fahrenheit 451—Books and beyond—A living legend—
In his own words.
ISBN 0-7660-2240-4 (hardcover)
1. Bradbury, Ray, 1920–   Juvenile literature. 2. Authors,
American—20th century—Biography—Juvenile literature. 3. Science
fiction—Authorship—Juvenile literature. 4. Fantasy
fiction—Authorship—Juvenile literature. [1. Bradbury, Ray, 1920–
2. Authors, American.] I. Title. II. Series.
PS3503.R167Z75   2003
813'.54—dc22

                                        2003012323

Printed in the United States of America

10 9 8 7 6 5 4 3 2

To Our Readers: We have done our best to make sure all Internet addresses in this book were active and appropriate when we went to press. However, the author and the publisher have no control over and assume no liability for the material available on those Internet sites or on other Web sites they may link to. Any comments or suggestions can be sent by e-mail to comments@enslow.com or to the address on the back cover.

Illustration Credits: AP/ Wide World Photos, pp. 8, 14, 21, 26, 30, 42, 62, 68, 72, 76, 78, 82; Enslow Publishers, Inc., pp. 32, 52, 58; Library of Congress, pp. 23, 36, 60; National Aeronautics and Space Administration (NASA), p. 50.

Cover Illustration: AP/ Wide World Photos (foreground); June Ponte (background).

Dedication

*For my good friend Andy Breckman,
who is living the dream.*

"Bradbury's stories, like many of his aliens, enter our minds and leave us, perhaps, subtly different from the way we were before."
—Wayne L. Johnson

CONTENTS

PREFACE

Ray Bradbury does not drive a car. Instead, he rides his bicycle or takes taxis around town. He refused to fly in an airplane until he was in his sixties. He does not use a computer or e-mail. Yet he has spent his life writing about the cars and flying machines and communication devices of the future. He is the master of asking, "What if?" He can look at an accident scene and ask, "What if the crowd that has suddenly gathered at the site of this car accident is the same crowd that gathers at the site of every accident?" Suddenly, a short story (in this case, "The Crowd") is born. Like six hundred others, it would be published and read by fans all over the world.

At twenty-three years old, Bradbury exclaimed, "There are plenty of good stories in everyday things. Trains, crowds, motor-cars, submarines, dogs—the wind around the house. . . . I want to write about humans; and add an unusual, unexpected twist."[2] Known as the Grand Master of science fiction, Bradbury argues that it is not a valid label: "I never wrote science fiction in my life, except for *Fahrenheit 451*. *The Martian Chronicles* is fantasy. Most of my short stories are fantasy. Science fiction is the art of the possible. Fantasy is the art of the impossible."[3] Science fiction writer Frederik Pohl agrees, saying that, "By and large, science fiction writers celebrate technology. Ray Bradbury does not. In his stories the gadgets and machines of the future are dehumanizing. Virtue lies in the simpler, gentler times of his midwestern childhood."[4]

More than simply tales of the fantastic, the bizarre, the unexpected, or the macabre, Bradbury's stories invite readers to look closely at themselves and the world in which they live. As Bradbury scholar Wayne L. Johnson puts it, "Bradbury's stories, like many of his aliens, enter our minds and leave us, perhaps, subtly different from the way we were before."[5]

One of the many things that sets him apart from other writers of speculative fiction is the mood he creates with his poetic choice of words. He makes a scene come to life and evokes all the senses. In the introduction to his collection of short stories *The October Country*, he explains that the October Country is " . . . that country where it is always turning late in the year. That country where the hills are fog and the rivers are mist; where noons go quickly, dusks and twilights linger, and midnights stay. That country composed in the

> "There are plenty of good stories in everyday things. Trains, crowds, motor-cars, submarines, dogs—the wind around the house. . . . I want to write about humans; and add an unusual, unexpected twist."
> —Ray Bradbury

main of cellars, sub-cellars, coal-bins, closets, attics, and pantries faced away from the sun. That country whose people are autumn people, thinking only autumn thoughts. Whose people passing at night on the empty walks sound like rain. . ."[6]

Ambitious and focused from a very young age, Bradbury was always fearless when it came to furthering his career. He is always willing to try different things, and to fully dedicate himself to the craft of writing and creating new worlds. This drive has led to his becoming the world's most anthologized writer, appearing in thousands of anthologies and text books.[7] Scholar David Mogen identifies a rough pattern in Bradbury's writing over the course of his career: He started in the 1940s and 1950s with straighter science fiction and fantasy, shifted to fantastical autobiography for the later 1950s and early 1960s, and went on to mystery/detective novels in the 1980s and 1990s.[8] He has published over thirty books, six hundred original short stories in magazines, and numerous plays, poems, essays, radio scripts, screenplays, and television scripts. He has even written two operas and several musicals.

A nearly perfect memory helps Bradbury to recall the things of childhood that most people forget. He even claims to remember being born. He wrote a story based on the experience called "The Small Assassin." It features a baby who is born fully aware of his situation and who takes revenge on his parents for bringing him into the world.

When Ray was little, he used to listen to a radio show called *Chandu the Magician* and then write out the entire script from memory. The young Midwestern boy who had "obsessions with Space, with magic, with Dracula at midnight and Frankenstein at noon,"[9] would become the man who would wind up enthralling readers for six decades. And he has not stopped yet.

> "I'm not a science fiction writer. I am a magician. I can use words to make you believe anything."[1]
> "I pretend to do one thing, cause you to blink, and in the instant seize 20 bright silks out of a bottomless hat."[2]
>
> —Ray Bradbury

Chapter 1

MEETING THE MAGICIANS

Two events in Ray's life changed it forever. They both had to do with magic. First, when Ray was eight years old, he came across a huge poster tacked up on a building wall. It was advertising the arrival of the famous magician, Harry Blackstone. Ray stood in front of that wall for an hour, staring in excitement. He knew that he had to be in that audience. When the night of the show arrived, Ray was there. Blackstone needed an assistant to help make an elephant disappear, and Ray made sure he was called on stage. As a gift,

Harry Blackstone was one of the most famous magicians of his time.

Blackstone gave him a rabbit to take home. He named it Tillie.

Ray was hooked on magic from that moment on and decided to be a magician. Sporting a cape and a fake mustache, Ray performed not only for his family and friends, but also at town functions and picnics. He saved up his money and bought magic tricks from carnivals or sent away for them from catalogues. Very often during a performance, his mustache would fall off or the trick would fail. Ray did not care. He loved being on stage and amazing people. He carried the tricks with him in his pocket in case the opportunity to perform arose. Forty years after they first met, Ray said, "Harry Blackstone pulled me out of a hat when I was a boy, and I have never stopped growing amidst mysteries, miracles, and dreams."[3]

A few years after Ray met Blackstone, a second magician entered his life. It was the Friday night before Labor Day in 1932. Twelve-year-old Ray attended a carnival on the shores of Lake Michigan, near his home. He sat in the front row while the amazing Mr. Electrico performed miraculous feats. The magician traveled with a homemade electric chair that he would sit on like it was a throne while "electricity" coursed through his body.

Sitting in the front row, Ray watched in awe. When the "electric current" was turned on, Ray saw the old man's white hair stand on end and sparks fly between his teeth. Then Mr. Electrico reached out and one by one, touched his sword to the brows of the exhilarated children. When the sword touched Ray, he could feel his own hair stand up and imagined that sparks flew out of his ears. Mr. Electrico then shouted the two words that Ray will never forget: "Live forever!"[4]

The next day was a sad one for Ray and his family. One of his favorite uncles had passed away and Ray attended the funeral in the morning. On the ride home, they passed the carnival tents. Ray knew that he had to find out the meaning behind Mr. Electrico's instructions. How did one live forever? He begged his father to stop the car and let him out. Mr. Bradbury reluctantly agreed and Ray jumped out, heading down the hill toward the tents. It was almost as if Mr. Electrico had known he was coming. The great magician greeted him warmly and Ray suddenly felt shy. He broke the ice by asking Mr. Electrico to show him how to do the magic trick he had purchased the night before, which he had with him. Ray was afraid to ask the real question on his mind.

> The great magician greeted him warmly and Ray suddenly felt shy.

After he demonstrated the trick, Mr. Electrico invited Ray to meet the other carnival folk. Ray met the Fat Lady, the Skeleton Man, the Illustrated Man, and many other strange performers. These characters left a lifelong impression and, in one way or another, they all eventually would wind up in his short stories.

Afterward, he walked with Mr. Electrico down to the lakefront and they sat on the sand to talk about life. After a while, Mr. Electrico told him that the two of them had met before. Ray gently insisted that they had not met before the previous night. Mr. Electrico told him, "You were my best friend in the great war in France in 1918 and you were wounded and died in my arms at the battle of the Ardennes Forest. But now, here today, I see his soul shining out of your eyes. Here you are, with a new face, a new name, but the soul shining from your face is the soul of my dear dead friend. Welcome back to the world."[5]

Ray knew that he had been given a great gift that day. He felt like he had awakened to life. Years later, in a fictionalized autobiography, Ray relayed what it was like for a twelve-year-old boy to come to the realization that he was alive. "The grass whispered under his body. He put his arm down, feeling the sheath of fuzz on it. . . . I want to feel all there is to feel, he thought. Let me feel tired, now, let me feel tired. I mustn't forget, I'm alive, I know I'm alive, I mustn't forget it tonight or tomorrow or the day after that."[6]

Ray learned from Mr. Electrico that he had lived before (whether it was true did not matter to him), and he decided that he would find a way to live forever. By writing stories, he could share the wonder he found in the world and, like a magician, he would bring amazing things to life and surprise people. A few days later, his family moved from Illinois to Tucson, Arizona, where they would live for less than a year. Ray began to write stories on a long roll of butcher paper. He has written every single day of his life since then, and credits Mr. Electrico for sparking his dreams and his ambition.

> "I was in love with everything I did. My heart did not beat, it exploded. I did not warm toward a subject, I boiled over. I have always run fast and yelled loud about a list of great magical things I knew I simply could not live without."[1]
>
> —Ray Bradbury

Chapter 2

THE WONDER YEARS

Raymond Douglas Bradbury was born on August 22, 1920 in Waukegan, Illinois. His middle name was a tribute to the actor Douglas Fairbanks, and reflected his mother's love of the movies. His parents, Leonard and Esther Bradbury, already had two sons, Leonard and Samuel, but Samuel had passed away before Ray was born. A daughter, Elizabeth, was born in 1926, but died the following year. At the time, Ray was only seven years

old. It was a few weeks before it sunk in that he was not going to see his sister again.

Waukegan was a slow-paced town off Lake Michigan, north of Chicago. To Ray, it seemed the most beautiful small town in the world. As a child, he did not notice the run-down areas and the unemployment. He loved the fact that he and his brother could play in the nearby ravine, and that so many of his relatives lived on the same block. He was friendly with a man who would also grow up to become a household name—actor Jack Benny, who had gone to school with Ray's mother. Benny used to play the violin in concert programs, and Ray would introduce him. Together they were called "The Boys from Waukegan."[2]

His mother's love of movies rubbed off on Ray. When he was three, she took him to see his first horror film, *The Hunchback of Notre Dame*, starring Lon Chaney.

When he was five, he saw *The Phantom of the Opera* and *The Lost World*. These movies, filled with mystery and magical beings, made a big impression on him. It was hard to say which he loved more—movies or books.

Ray's favorite books were about fantastic adventures and other worlds. His young Aunt Neva—short for Nevada—lived right next door. She was a costume designer and made him masks and puppets and Halloween costumes. Through her, he developed his love for Halloween and for that time of year in general. He says that Halloween is his favorite holiday because "it has

Jack Benny was a comedian whose career spanned the early
days of vaudeville and radio and lasted into the days of
television and movies.

to do with life and death, with the end of things and with the possibility of new beginnings."[3] Neva expanded his imagination in other ways, too. She read him *Alice in Wonderland* by Lewis Carroll, works by Edgar Allen Poe, and Grimm's *Fairy Tales*. On his own, he pored through the *Oz* books by L. Frank Baum, the *Buck Rogers* comics, the *Tarzan* books, and anything by Jules Verne and H. G. Wells. He discovered the science fiction (SF) magazine *Amazing Stories* when he was eight. He was encouraged by his family to read the Greek, Roman, and Norse myths, along with the Bible. These were the stories that fed Ray's imagination. According to scholar David Mogen, "His immersion in popular culture began at three," and grew to include "a wide variety of entertainment media: books, comics, movies, theater, museums, magic-shows, circuses."[4]

Ray visited the library three or four times a week. "I hid out there summers, hiding from bullies," he explained. "They didn't like you if you were bright. I didn't know I was bright then. I discovered that later. But they could smell it on me."[5]

Ray did not need to travel far to find inspiration. To him, the world was surrounded by wonder. The bright sunlight brought dark imaginings. Creaks in the walls meant ghosts in the attic. The ravine was full of danger; carnival lights meant that magic had come to town. He let everyday objects and events seep into him so that the world around him always felt alive and full of possibilities.

This famous Depression-era photograph by Dorothea Lange captured the suffering endured by those who lived through the period.

Due to the Great Depression in the 1930s, jobs were scarce. Ray's father found it difficult to hold onto a steady job as a telephone lineman. When Ray was six, his father moved the family to Tucson, Arizona. They soon returned to Waukegan, however, and back to the same block where so many of Ray's family members lived.

Ray's brother Leonard (whose nickname was Skip) was athletic and played sports, but Ray knew that his own loves lay elsewhere. He began

> ## "I hid out there [in the library] summers, hiding from bullies"
> ### —Ray Bradbury

collecting comic strips about an intergalactic crime fighter named Buck Rogers when he was nine, until the boys at school started making fun of him. To prove that he did not care about the comic strips, he tore them up. Later, as the tears kept coming, he realized that he had destroyed something he had really cared about. He decided never to let anyone else's opinion affect him; he would keep following his passions. He began collecting *Buck Rogers* comics again, and later he would add *Tarzan*, *Flash Gordon*, *Prince Valiant*, and many more.

At twelve, his family moved back to Tucson because his father needed to find work. Although they would again stay there less than a year, it was a big year for Ray. Chosen to sing in the Christmas pageant at school, he solidified his love of being on stage. It would soon conflict with another love, though—writing. As a Christmas present that year, Ray received a toy typewriter. He immediately started writing his own stories based on *Buck Rogers* and Edgar Rice Burroughs's character John Carter of Mars (which later would inspire his own *Martian Chronicles*). He also found his first job. A local radio station hired him to read comic strips over the air on Saturday mornings. He was overjoyed. His payment was free tickets to horror movies like *King Kong, The Mummy*, and *Murders in the Wax Museum*.

A turning point for Ray in terms of spirituality and religion happened when he and his brother read in the local paper that the world would end at noon the next day, May 24. So he and Skip got up early, packed a huge picnic lunch, and hiked to the top of a hill to get a good view. They were not sure what to expect, but decided that it probably would not be a flood. By four o'clock, they were sufficiently sick to their stomachs from all the food they ate and upset that the world had not ended after all. Ray decided then that the world would end when his own life did, so in the meantime he might as well keep on living and trying to do good things.[6]

Now back in Waukegan, Ray's Aunt Neva brought him to Chicago to attend the 1933 World's Fair. His favorite exhibit was the City of the Future section of the Century of Progress

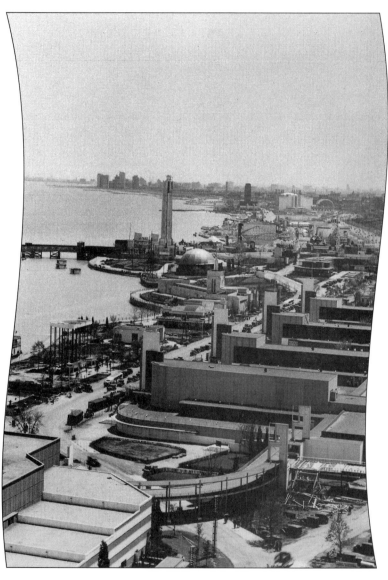

This is a view of the 1933 World's Fair, as seen from the top of the skyride.

exhibit. He was so enthralled with the buildings that he had to be physically dragged away. He could not believe that the Fair was going to be torn down in a few years. He dreamed that some day he would help design those cities of the future. And he would—but not for many years.

Chapter 3

HOORAY FOR Hollywood

When Ray was fourteen, his family moved to Los Angeles, California. His father had gotten a steady job and the family found an apartment near Hollywood. This time, the move would be permanent. As much as Ray had loved Waukegan, Hollywood was the place where dreams came alive. Ray's childhood love of the movies only blossomed.

Picked on at his new school for being bookish and shy, he was anything but that out of school.

He befriended neighborhood movie theater owners, who let him sneak in to the shows. Sometimes he saw five or six movies a week. He was fascinated by the movie stars he would see around Hollywood. After school, he would strap on his roller skates and skate through the studios in search of famous people. Ray loved collecting autographs and was thrilled each time he got someone famous to sign his autograph book or to pose for a picture with him. For weeks he followed comedian George Burns around town, slipping him ideas for his popular "Burns and Allen" radio show. Finally, Burns agreed to use a few lines that Ray wrote to close the radio show and Ray was ecstatic.

Because he loved performing on the stage, Ray decided he wanted to become an actor and joined the drama club at school. But when his teachers saw what a talented writer he was, they convinced him to focus on writing instead. He compromised by writing the skits for the school's talent show, which he also directed. He wrote for the school newspaper and joined the poetry club, too. While Ray loved reading and learning about a wide range of things, the only subject he worked hard at was writing. Math was his worst subject. The two English teachers who helped his talent bloom became his lifelong friends.

At seventeen, Ray joined the Los Angeles Science Fiction League. This group of established and aspiring writers was just what Ray needed to inspire his writing. He befriended some of

George Burns was a legendary comedian who was best known for his radio show, "Burns and Allen," and his starring roles in the *Oh, God!* movies.

the most important writers in the field, including the already well-known science fiction writer Robert Heinlein. These people worked closely with Ray and encouraged him to find his own voice. Ray explains that "from the time I was 12 until I was 22 or 23, I wrote stories long after midnight—unconventional stories of ghosts and haunts and things in jars that I had seen in sour armpit carnivals, of friends lost to the tides in lakes, and of consorts of three in the morning, those souls who had to fly in the dark in order not to be shot in the sun."[2] He was finding his voice, his unique rhythm.

One member of the League was Forrest J. Ackerman. The two became close friends. Ackerman lovingly described Ray: "He was loud, boisterous, always hamming it up with impersonations. . . . How lucky that we didn't strangle him and rob the world of one of the greatest literary talents and socially stimulating individuals of the twentieth century."[3]

Ackerman become famous as a science fiction writer, an editor of SF and monster magazines, an agent for other SF writers, and a huge collector of SF memorabilia. He is still one of Ray Bradbury's closest friends. Through him, eighteen-year-old Ray met another lifelong friend and fellow science fiction/fantasy/horror film fanatic, Ray Harryhausen. Whereas Ray Bradbury was on the writing end of the process, Harryhausen was a special effects buff who grew up creating models of dinosaurs in his garage. No wonder the two hit

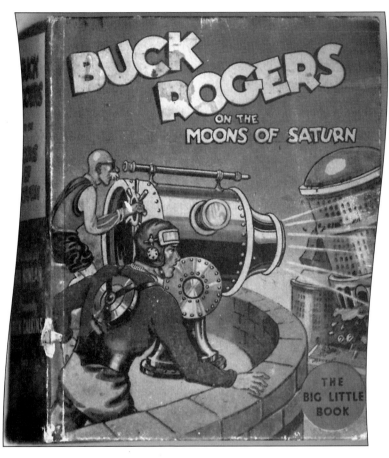

Comic-strip heroes such as *Buck Rogers* captivated Ray Bradbury as a child.

it off so well! Ray Bradbury says, "We promised each other we'd always love dinosaurs. We'd grow old but never grow up."[4] At the 1992 Oscar awards, Ray Bradbury had the honor of presenting his close friend with the Lifetime Achievement Award for bringing movie special effects and animation to a new level of greatness and inspiring all those who came after him. "I was proud of myself for keeping our love intact," Ray Bradbury said. "That changed my life."[5]

Unable to afford college, Ray's post–high school education consisted of reading everything he could get his hands on. The public library and local bookstores became his university. He got his first paying job selling newspapers on a street corner in Los Angeles for ten dollars a week. This schedule allowed him time to write stories and read books in the library at night. He read everything from the classics to very obscure works, and took a class on short story writing. His family now lived near the beach and his brother played semi-professional football.

In his late teens, Ray was immersed in the "fandom" scene, which was made up of groups of SF and fantasy writers who created their own handmade magazines called fanzines. New writers were encouraged to submit their work or to put out their own magazines. The fans wrote letters to the editors of these magazines, giving their opinions on the stories. It was a thriving subculture. Ray wrote letters and published some stories and columns in various fanzines. His first published story, "Hollerbochen's Dilemma," appeared in 1938 in a fanzine called *Imagination!*, which was put out by the Science Fiction League. To see more of his work in print, Ray decided that he needed to put out his own fanzine. With a borrowed mimeograph machine (the precursor to the copy machine), he printed *Futuria Fantasia* in 1939. It was very expensive and time consuming, so he only put out four issues.

> **In his late teens, Ray was immersed in the "fandom" scene, which was made up of groups of SF and fantasy writers who created their own handmade magazines called fanzines.**

That same year, the first World Science Fiction Convention was being held in New York City. Many of the major players in the science fiction book, magazine, and movie world would be at the convention (known as NYCon), along with dedicated fans of the genre. Ray desperately wanted to go, but could not afford it. His friend Forrest J. Ackerman volunteered to loan him the fifty dollars it would cost to get him there on the train. He accepted Ackerman's offer and was forever grateful. At the conference, Ray and his friends attended lectures on various SF-related topics and attended gatherings where people dressed up in costumes from their favorite SF movies. Ray recalls the weekend as one of the best times of his life.[6]

At twenty, Ray Bradbury's first short story was published in a very well-respected magazine called *Script*, put out by editor Rob Wagner. The story was a comedic tale called "It's Not the Heat It's the Hu. . ." The magazine was published locally in Beverly Hills. Although he was not paid any money for the story, he was very excited just to get free copies of the magazine.

The next step up the publishing ladder was the "pulp" magazines (the name refers to the low-quality, inexpensive paper on which the magazines were printed). These included titles like *Weird Tales*, *Thrilling Wonder Stories*, and *Planet Stories*. Ray Bradbury began sending his stories to these "pulps," which specialized in SF, fantasy, adventure, horror, and the supernatural. The authors were paid between twenty and forty dollars a story.

Success was not far away. At twenty-one years of age, after nearly ten years of practice, Ray Bradbury published his first paying short story in *Super Science Stories* in 1941. "Pendulum" was a collaboration between himself and his friend Henry Hasse, an established SF writer. The story was about a man convicted of a crime being imprisoned in a giant pendulum. That way, he was doomed to move through time as he served time.

The famous film *King Kong* was a favorite of Ray Bradbury when he was young.

Spurred on by his accomplishment (and his half of the $27.50 payment), Ray Bradbury began the word-association writing technique that he still uses today. He wrote down lists of unconnected nouns on a piece of paper—words like "the Lake," "the Night," "the Crickets," "the Ravine," "the Attic," "the Carnival," "the Dwarf," and "the Skeleton." He then looked over the list and found that the nouns were like pieces of a puzzle he could fit together. These random words brought up childhood memories, old loves, and old fears he had forgotten about. He began typing. Out of that first list came a story called "The Lake." Ray describes the experience as life-changing:

> I wrote the story sitting outside, with my typewriter, on the lawn. At the end of an hour, the story was finished, the hair on the back of my neck was standing up, and I was in tears. I knew I had written the first really good story of my life.[7]

"The Lake" eventually sold to *Weird Tales* for twenty dollars, although the publishers were not thrilled with its nontraditional nature. It just did not fit into any clear category. Ray Bradbury would often hear that complaint early on in his career, when most writers of his genre were producing straight horror, SF, or fantasy—not all three at once.

Some of the nouns on Bradbury's list would remain there for decades, until the story rose up inside him and he ran to write it down. In 1941 alone, he wrote fifty-two stories. Three of them were sold to the pulp magazines. In 1942, he sold a handful more. By 1943, he had sold a dozen stories. He finally had the courage to quit his job selling newspapers, and rented an office in a tenement building so he could write while still living at home with his parents.

He was now a full-time writer.

"The sheer lift and power of a truly original imagination exhilarates you, almost in spite of yourself. So I urge even the most squeamish to try Mr. Bradbury. His is a very great and unusual talent."[1]

—Christopher Isherwood, book reviewer

"I write for fun . . . I approach my craft with enthusiasm and respect. If my work sparks serious thought, fine. But I don't write with that in mind. I'm not a serious person, and I don't like serious people. . . . My goal is to entertain myself and others."[2]

—Ray Bradbury

Chapter 4

Bradbury's Early Career and Marriage

Now relying solely on the sales of his stories to bring him money, Bradbury knew he could not slow his pace. He continued to write every day and his output of stories was extraordinary. Although his bad eyesight kept him from serving in World War II, he helped the war effort by writing radio announcements for the Red Cross and other material for the Los Angeles Department of Civil Defense. In 1944, he sold forty stories to the pulp magazines, including mystery pulps like *Detective Tales* and *Dime Mystery*. It was time to climb one more rung up the publishing ladder. The following year, Bradbury began sending his work to the "slick" magazines, which, like the pulps, got their name from the heavier, glossier paper on which they were printed. These included *Charm*, *Mademoiselle*, *Collier's*, and *Cosmopolitan*. The slick magazines were sold in many more places and were considered more "mainstream," in that they included stories and articles geared more toward the interests of the general population.

At first, Bradbury sent his stories under a fake name because he feared that the slicks would not want to publish someone who was already known for publishing in the pulps. But when the editors surprised him and bought the stories, he quickly told them who he really was. Bradbury became the only science fiction writer of that time to have made the leap from pulp magazines to mainstream publications. This was an occasion where the fact that he did not write purely science fiction, or purely horror, or purely mystery helped. The editors felt that he could appeal to a mainstream audience because his stories offered something for everyone. For such a young person, he had an incredible ability to understand and depict the human character.

Bradbury's first nationwide recognition came in 1945, when his story "The Black and White

Game" was selected to be in the anthology *Best American Short Stories*. It had been a major goal of his to be included in the well-respected collection, so this was a big step for him. Soon after, he would take an even bigger leap—he would fall in love.

In 1946, Bradbury was browsing in one of his favorite bookstores in downtown Los Angeles. There he met Marguerite (Maggie) McClure, a young woman who worked there. She had been told by her boss to be on the lookout for shoplifters, and when Bradbury walked in with a briefcase and a long coat, she began watching him suspiciously. He got up the nerve to talk to her, and the two

> **Bradbury continued to write every day and his output of stories was extraordinary.**

started dating. Her friends warned her not to marry him, saying that he was not going to amount to anything. But Bradbury would not give up. Bradbury says that he told Maggie, "I'm going to the moon. You want to come along? And she said yes. And that's the best yes I ever heard in my life. Turned out to be just right."[3]

They married a year later, on September 27, 1947, with Ray Harryhausen as the best man. They made a great pair. Maggie had gone to UCLA and was often her husband's first reader. Later she would become a professor. They had just ten dollars in the bank when they first got married, but luckily that same year Bradbury's first collection

Ray Bradbury (above) had his first collection of short stories published in 1947.

of short stories, *Dark Carnival*, was published. He also won his first big honor—the O. Henry Award for a short story named "Homecoming."

The Bradburys' first home was a small house in Venice, California. Maggie went to work while Bradbury wrote and took care of housework. An event that happened on the beach one night is an example of how Bradbury does not find his ideas—they find him. The young newlyweds loved to walk on the nearby beach together. They were strolling one night when up ahead they saw the ruins of an old roller coaster. With Bradbury's imagination running overtime as usual, he asked his wife what a dinosaur was doing lying on the beach. Later that night, he heard a foghorn blowing out over the ocean and suddenly he knew: The dinosaur had thought that the sound of the foghorn was another dinosaur, had gone looking for it, and had died of a broken heart. The next morning Bradbury wrote "The Fog Horn" and sent it off to the *Saturday Evening Post*. It was soon published under the title "The Beast From 20,000 Fathoms." The story was his first big sale, and its publication would bring him many even bigger opportunities.

As proved by his early success with the slick magazines, Bradbury began to submit his stories to places not known for publishing his type of fiction, or even fiction at all. He had a theory that editors were so tired of seeing the same type of articles over and over, that something fresh might excite them. He sent one of the stories that would later appear in *Dandelion Wine* to a cooking magazine called *Gourmet*, which had no history of publishing fiction. Surprisingly, it was accepted. Bradbury's clever gamble paid off and he continued to publish in unexpected places.[4]

A distinct literary approach was beginning to emerge from Bradbury's stories. He had developed his own unique method of pulling the reader into the story and assuring that the reader remembers the story long after he or she closes the book. One

> A distinct literary approach was beginning to emerge from Bradbury's stories. He had developed his own unique method of pulling the reader into the story.

of the ways he achieves this is with his use of metaphors and similes. He reveals the essence of something by describing it in the context of something else. For example, in "The Fog Horn," he describes the dinosaur as a "great evil god." This lets the reader know that the beast is very powerful and frightful without having to use those adjectives, and by doing so, strengthens the image in the reader's mind.

The times when this tactic works best is when Bradbury uses metaphors or similes that force the reader to use his or her imagination to complete the picture. Scholar Wayne L. Johnson gives an example from the same story. The inventor of the foghorn is explaining what the horn will sound like when he builds it. He says, "I'll make a voice that is like an empty bed beside you all night long, and like an empty house when you open the door, and like trees in autumn with no leaves."[5] Each reader has to imagine what those concepts would "sound" like, or what they would "feel" like on an emotional level. Each reader is forced to draw from his or her own experiences of such occasions. As Johnson concludes, "It is the experiential aspect of Bradbury's stories, the feeling that something has *happened* to the reader, that is perhaps their outstanding feature. The effect is achieved through the generation of strong sensory images, sensations of sight, touch, or sound. . ."[6]

In 1949, with his first daughter on the way, Bradbury turned toward focusing his efforts on book-length projects. This took him first to New York City, then all the way to Mars.

> "What gives the Martian Chronicles their cunning is . . . their portrayal of human nature, in all its baseness and all its promise, against an exquisite stage-set. We are shown normality, the permanent things in human nature, by the light of another world; and what we forget about ourselves in the ordinariness of our routine of existence suddenly bursts upon us as fresh revelation . . . Bradbury's stories are not an escape from reality; they are windows looking upon enduring reality." [1]

Chapter 5

THE MARTIAN CHRONICLES

Inspired by the way author Sherwood Anderson created a world out of the everyday lives of his characters in *Winesburg, Ohio*, Bradbury knew he wanted to create such a world—but on Mars. He began jotting down ideas that were not yet stories, just small scenes or images of different elements of the life on Mars—the architecture, the food, weather, and so on. Then, when he could truly visualize the environment, he gradually built stories around them.[2]

Bradbury kept hearing how hard it was to sell a collection of stories. In 1949, Norman Corwin, a radio host and trusted friend, encouraged him to travel to New York City to meet with editors so they would get to know him personally. Bradbury agreed and took a bus (with no air conditioning) four days and four nights across the country. He met with various editors, but as expected, no one was interested in a short story collection. One of the editors at Doubleday—a man named Walter Bradbury (no relation)—suggested that he turn his short stories about Mars into a novel. That night, Bradbury returned to the YMCA where he was staying and looked over the short stories he had written between 1944 and 1949. He shuffled them around and wrote small "bridge-like" chapters to link the stories together. The result was *The Martian Chronicles*. Walter Bradbury thought it was perfect and asked if he had any other stories he could do the same thing with. Bradbury returned to the YMCA and put together another batch of stories, which became *The Illustrated Man*. Bradbury was paid $750 for each book. He was thrilled. That $1,500 paid for two years of rent and greatly eased his family's financial burden. In those days, the literary community did not take science fiction very seriously, and only a few novels were published each year. So to have sold two at the same time was a huge accomplishment.

Even with the added transitions, the twenty-six

chapters in *The Martian Chronicles* are fairly disjointed, because they were originally intended to stand on their own. There are no central characters in the book, although a few show up in more than one story. Bradbury organized the stories in such a way as to show a progression of events over a period of twenty-seven years. That way, the book feels like it has a beginning, middle, and an end. He had originally used the year 1999 as the beginning of the colonization of Mars, but when the present recently caught up with the future, he changed the date to 2050 for a new edition.

The book focuses on Earth's attempt to colonize Mars, the effects on the Martian population, and the colonists' reaction to nuclear war back home. The stories reflect the anxieties of the 1950s—the threat of nuclear war, the sudden complexity of modern living,

> Doubleday editor Walter Bradbury suggested he turn his short stories about Mars into a novel.

a growing racism, and a fear of foreign powers. One journalist dubbed it "social commentary set in outer space."[3] It is the story of a new frontier. Together, the stories illustrate the mistakes the settlers can make, the importance of recognizing other cultures, and the need to adapt to new environments. It is also a warning of what could happen when colonization goes unchecked. As in all of his stories, his descriptions of the physical beauty of places the travelers encounter are skillfully and lovingly rendered.

In the beginning, the Martians easily trick the first groups of Earthmen that come to Mars. Able to read their minds telepathically, the Martians know the Earth people's weaknesses. They feel threatened by this perceived invasion of their planet and take swift action. The crew of the first ship to land is shot to death because a Martian fears that his wife might fall in love with one of them. Long-lost friends and family members who supposedly had died long ago greet another ship. Even their old houses seem to be there, on Mars. The crew is lured to their old homes and killed. It turns out that the Martians had recreated the entire scene. The next few invasions are more successful. Eventually, towns are built with supplies from Earth as the humans try to recreate what they left behind. Most of the Martians eventually die from diseases the Earth people bring with them. The rest live on the outskirts of the towns in the mountains. Then, there is nuclear war on Earth. Most of the new settlers return home to help out. The remaining Earthmen—and the new arrivals who flee the war—must deal with the fact that they are now the new Martians. They had to undergo a metamorphosis—from Earthmen into Martians—as the only way to survive.

The idea of metamorphosis, of changing from one thing into something else, is a common theme in Bradbury's writing. In *Voices for the Future:*

An artist's depiction of an imagined future landing on the planet Mars.

Essays on Major Science Fiction Writers, A. James Stupple writes:

> Bradbury's point here is clear: [The Earthmen] met their deaths because of their inability to forget, or at least resist, the past. Thus, the story of this Third Expedition acts as a metaphor for the book as a whole. Again and again the Earthmen make the fatal mistake of trying to recreate an Earth-like past rather than accept the fact that this is Mars—a different, unique new land in which they must be ready to make personal adjustments.[4]

Not long after the book was published, Bradbury was in a bookstore. He recognized Christopher Isherwood, a highly respected literary critic. Never one to let an opportunity pass him by, Bradbury pulled a copy of *The Martian Chronicles* off the shelf and handed it to Isherwood. Isherwood was not very excited to read it. Science fiction books were not often reviewed or taken very seriously. They were almost never reported on by the mainstream reviewers. But Isherwood agreed to take the book home and wound up loving it. He then wrote a rave review of it, which not only increased its sales, but also boosted the reputation of the entire science fiction genre. Isherwood praised the plot of the book along with the lyrical, metaphorical writing itself. His review discussed the fact that unlike most other science fiction, *The Martian Chronicles* did not include many technical, scientific terms that often weighed down other books in that genre. By taking a science fiction writer seriously, he helped make Bradbury's name a respected one and the

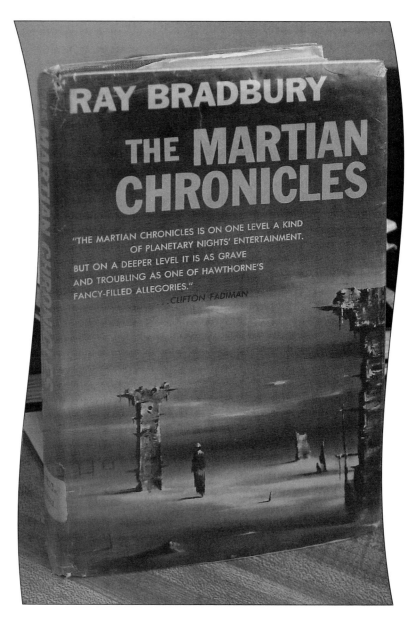

Cover of *The Martian Chronicles*

book a best seller that has never been out of print. Nearly fifty years later, a new generation of literary scholars agree that Bradbury's poetic writing in *The Martian Chronicles* still shines. "Full grown without memory, the robots waited. In green silks the color of forest pools, in silks the color of frog and fern, they waited." *The Martian Chronicles* are full of such stuff—lyrical, dreamlike, ethereal.[5]

Even though Bradbury's *The Martian Chronicles* was a big step toward legitimizing science fiction, the book does not uphold many of the rules of the genre. Bradbury's spaceships did not mimic the space shuttles that really travel to space. Nor did his Mars reflect the reality of the fourth planet from the sun. There is no breathable atmosphere on Mars, for instance. He admits that his Mars is a fantasy, a myth. He believes that is why the book has had such long life.[6] The only story in it that he considers science fiction is "There Will Come Soft Rains," which tells the tale of a house that lives on by itself when its inhabitants have perished in a nuclear war.

The book has had a very long life, and has mutated into many forms. In addition to numerous stage plays based on the stories, a television miniseries was broadcast in 1980. Fifty years after it was published, there is now a computer game based on *The Martian Chronicles* to which Bradbury has given his stamp of approval.

In 1951, right on the heels of *The Martian Chronicles*, came *The Illustrated Man*. The unifying theme of this collection of short stories was that a man's tattoos came to life when he went to sleep at night. Each chapter told the story that was illustrated in one of the tattoos. The book was well received, but would soon be overshadowed by Bradbury's first novel and what many consider his greatest work, *Fahrenheit 451*.

> "(When I was a child) I used to memorize entire books. I suppose that's where the ending of *Fahrenheit 451* comes from—where the book people wander through the wilderness and each of them is a book. That was me when I was ten. I was *Tarzan of the Apes*." [1]
>
> —Ray Bradbury

Chapter 6

FAHRENHEIT 451

By 1952, Bradbury's name was so well known that he was elected president of the newly formed Science Fiction and Fantasy Writers of America. The next year he published the only book that would rival the fame of *The Martian Chronicles*. *Fahrenheit 451*, named after the temperature at which paper burns, was based on a short novella called "The Fireman," which Bradbury published in *Galaxy* magazine in 1951. When Bradbury sat down to write the novella, he found that his life at home (he now had two young daughters) was too hectic for him to concentrate. He discovered that in the basement of the UCLA library, he could rent a typewriter for ten cents an hour. For nine days, he typed away madly as the clock ticked down each dime. Nine dollars and eighty cents later, he was finished. Soon after, he turned it into a novel, renaming it *Fahrenheit 451*.

Until that point, he had never written anything as long as a novel. He explained, "People think you can plot a novel, but you can't. You have to let people live. If they lead big lives, you've got a novel. If they lead small ones, you've got a short story."[2] When asked how the novel differed from the shorter version, Bradbury explained:

> It's inflated. The texture of it grew. I retyped "The Fireman" and as I went I added texture, line-by-line, character by character, idea by idea. It was a process I often go through with a poem. I don't revise, I retype, and as I'm going through, retyping the lines, things come to me, and my brain suggests, "Not that word, this one. Not that line, another line." It's an interior process growing outward through the words.[3]

Fahrenheit 451 is the story of a thirty-one-year-old firefighter named Guy Montag. Montag's job is to burn books in a future society where reading is illegal. People do not sit around and talk to each other anymore; rather, they stare transfixed at their "television walls" which pipe a constant stream of lowbrow entertainment into every household. One day, Montag meets an unusual young girl named Clarissa, who has moved in next door. She reminds him that he has lost touch with his humanity. He never thinks for himself anymore; he never looks around at the beauty of nature. He is not sure if he remembers that dew gathers on the early-morning grass. He knows he does not remember how he and his wife originally met each other, although it was only ten years before. He cannot tell if he is happy or not. He realizes that he needs to know the information hidden inside all those books he has been burning. One by one, he starts stealing books and hiding

> "People think you can plot a novel, but you can't. You have to let people live. If they lead big lives, you've got a novel. If they lead small ones, you've got a short story."
> —Ray Bradbury

them. He meets up with an old man who was once a professor, and together they make a plan to start changing the way society views books. Their plan quickly gets out of hand—leaving the fire chief dead and Montag's own house burned down. Montag runs for his life and winds up joining a band of rebels who live on the outskirts of the city. Each of the rebels has memorized a different book and they recite them to each other.

To drive home certain themes in the book, Bradbury quotes from a wide range of literature.

"The Fireman," the short story that Bradbury would later expand into *Farenheit 451*, first appeared in the February 1951 issue of *Galaxy* magazine (above).

The fact that he wrote the book in a library allowed him to keep running up and down the stairs to find what he needed. The quotes include passages from *Gulliver's Travels* by Jonathan Swift, *Boswell's Life of Johnson*, Shakespeare, John Donne, and Mathew Arnold's *Dover Beach*. Each passage helps Montag understand some of life's basic truths. Four biblical allusions underscore Bradbury's message that life moves in cycles. After dark times, there comes light again. The fire at the start of the book was only used to destroy, but at the end becomes a giver of life as Montag warms his hands over it. As in mythology, the phoenix (as represented on the fire helmets) will again rise from the ashes of this burnt civilization and knowledge will flourish. The book ends on a note of hope.

The novel was written during the time in history known now as the McCarthy Era. Writers were being accused of trying to subvert the government through their words. Free speech was threatened and books were taken off shelves. Bradbury was infuriated by what was going on around him, and *Fahrenheit 451* is partly a response to that. A philosophical work of science fiction and social criticism, the book is a commentary on censorship and the loss of personal freedom in the name of progress. It is a powerful statement on the ability of the printed word to inform, enlighten, educate, and heal. It is also a clear warning of the dangers of letting the media and the government invade people's lives. The characters in *Fahrenheit 451*

Senator Joseph McCarthy (above) and the advent of McCarthyism would inspire Ray Bradbury to write his novel, *Farenheit 451*.

are afraid to know what the world is really about. They are apathetic about life; they just do not care about anything. They trust the government to deal with everything for them so they do not have to think or worry too much. This unwillingness to face reality leads to their eventual ruin as bombs destroy the cities in a war they were busy ignoring.

In 1967, Bradbury's publisher released an edition of the book aimed at high school readers. They edited out any references to drinking and other behaviors and words not considered appropriate. Thus, a book about censorship had been censored. Fortunately, the original, unaltered version was still being published. But then in 1973, only the revised version was available for publication. This went on for six years until Bradbury was alerted to it by some students. He was horrified and made sure that the text was immediately restored to the original. In total, the editors had made ninety-eight changes.[4]

Fahrenheit 451 still resonates strongly today. Many of the things about life in Bradbury's imagined future have come true. The little radio earphones Bradbury called "seashells" in the book achieved reality when an inventor built the Sony Walkman. The kind of "virtual reality" that existed in the interactive televisions in Montag's living room is now a reality. The media really has invaded all aspects of life today. And unfortunately, the following passage about how books have fared in our fast-paced society rings true today, as well:

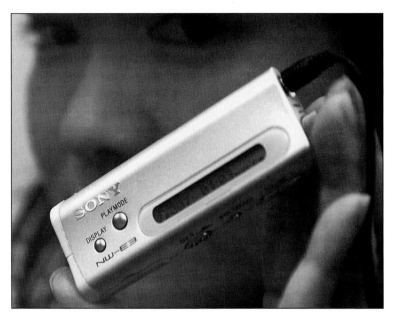

It pleases Ray Bradbury when technology, such as this Sony Walkman, catches up to the items he describes in his stories.

"Picture it. Nineteenth-century man with his horses, dogs, carts, slow motion. Then in the twentieth-century, speed up your camera. Books cut shorter. Condensations. Digests. Tabloids. Everything boils down to the gag, the snap ending. Classics cut to fit fifteen-minute radio shows. . . winding up at last as a ten or twelve-line diction-ary resume [entry]."[5] In the world of the novel, that was the fire chief's justification for why books became first ignored. It was later that they became dangerous.

In 2002, the mayor of Los Angles selected *Fahrenheit 451* for the "One Book, One City L.A." program. He encouraged all city residents to read the book. Many citywide activities were planned around it, including discussion groups and theater productions. The book's publisher donated five hundred copies and the libraries and bookstores stocked up, too. Palm Beach County, Florida, also selected the book for their citywide reading program. When asked if he is surprised by how much of the future he correctly predicted in the book, Bradbury replied, "I don't try to predict the future, I try to prevent it."[6]

"I've read every important play in the history of the world. It wasn't a job, it was a delight. I've read a certain amount of philosophy, psychology, art history. I've studied Shakespeare, the Bible, astronomy, city planning, architecture, rapid transit, poetry, the history of film. I've read all the important books on writing. I became a library person a long time ago, and in doing so I overcame that feeling of inferiority, that fear of not being capable."[1]

—Ray Bradbury

Chapter 7

Books and Beyond

By the time all four of his daughters had been born (Susan in 1949, Ramona in 1951, Bettina in 1955, and Alexandra in 1958), Bradbury was fast becoming a household name. He continued publishing short stories in major magazines and then releasing collections of them every few years. *The Martian Chronicles* (1950) and *Fahrenheit 451* (1953) are his best-known pieces of fiction, but they are quickly followed in popularity by *The*

Illustrated Man (1951), *Something Wicked This Way Comes* (1962), and *Dandelion Wine* (1957). The last two are considered "autobiographical fantasies." Bradbury took events from his own life growing up in Waukegan, Illinois (which in both books he calls Green Town), and then either idealized them or made them darker and more sinister.

Dandelion Wine was published first. It is the story of a young boy's awakening to life during one Midwestern summer. Impressed with the book's wistful and evocative tone, scholar Harold Bloom called it "a nostalgic paean to childhood innocence and imagination."[2] In contrast, *Something Wicked This Way Comes* is "the dark autumn" to *Dandelion Wine*'s "bright summer." In this novel, a father must save the souls of his son and his son's best friend from the evil clutches of a mysterious carnival.

Even as his stories were being published in a constant stream, Bradbury was involving himself in other forms of media. From April 1950 to September 1951, a weekly national radio show called *Dimension X* began adapting science fiction stories. Every few weeks, a new short story of Bradbury's would be broadcast, including "There Will Come Soft Rains" and "The Veldt." These radio adaptations captured the true spirit of Bradbury's stories. They also introduced his work to a broader audience, who might not have discovered him through his magazine publications. Also in the early fifties, many of his short stories were made into comic books. Because Ray was such a huge fan of comics, he was delighted with this turn of events. Although some people in the literary field looked down on comic books, Bradbury knew that, like his radio shows, they brought his work into the hands of people who might not otherwise have found it.

Beginning in the fifties and continuing into the nineties, Bradbury wrote original television episodes and adapted his own stories for *Alfred Hitchcock Presents* and *The Twilight Zone*. He later adapted sixty-five of his stories for the popular *Ray Bradbury Theatre*, which ran on television from May 1985 to October 1992 and can still be caught in reruns. The show was awarded numerous Cable Ace awards, the cable television version of the Emmy award. Bradbury wrote the scripts for each episode and he personally introduced them. In 1994, he won an Emmy for the Best Animated Children's Program for the television special based on his book, *The Halloween Tree*.

> "[*Dandelion Wine* is] a nostalgic paean to childhood innocence and imagination."
> —Harold Bloom

As someone who loved movies so much, Bradbury did not wait too long to try his hand at the medium. In 1952, Warner Brothers Studio bought the rights to adapt his story "The Beast from 20,000 Fathoms." They wound up using hardly anything from his story. Rather, they turned it into a monster movie, when it was really all about unrequited love. The good thing to come out of the experience was that Bradbury got to work with his old friend Ray Harryhausen. That same year, he was asked to write the treatment for a screenplay about aliens from outer space. Bradbury was so excited about what he wrote that he handed in almost a full script. *It Came from Outer Space* was the first three-dimensional (3-D) science fiction film, and it became a fan favorite. Decades later, when Bradbury met Steven Spielberg at the premiere of *Close Encounters of the Third Kind*, Spielberg told him that *It Came from Outer Space*, which he had seen six times as a child, was the inspiration for *Close Encounters*.[3]

In 1953, a famous movie director named John Huston asked Bradbury to write the movie version of *Moby Dick*. Huston had read the short story version of "The Beast from 20,000 Fathoms" and thought that Bradbury would be the perfect choice to convey the tone of Herman Melville's novel. Bradbury agreed, even though it meant moving his whole family to Ireland for six months. While it turned out to be good experience in terms of learning the screenwriting process, he and Huston were often at odds. In the end, Huston insisted on sharing writing credit on the film, which Bradbury did not think was fair.

In 1962, Bradbury was nominated for an Oscar for his animated short film on the history of flight, *Icarus Montgolfier Wright*. In 1966, a film producer named François Truffaut made a movie

It took director John Huston three years to get the movie adaptation of *Moby Dick* he co-wrote with Ray Bradbury to the screen.

version of *Fahrenheit 451*. By choice, Bradbury was not involved in much of the decision-making. Although he thought that while the director added many good things and he loved the ending, he felt that some important elements of the book's plot were left out. He also feared that the director's decision to have one actress—Julie Christie—play both of the female roles was confusing to the audience. He was much happier with that movie, however, than with *The Illustrated Man*, which was made into a film a few years later in 1969. He was not given any input on the project and felt that it departed too much from the book—and did not make a lot of sense. He felt similarly about the 1980 television miniseries of *The Martian Chronicles*. The attempt to tie all the stories into one overall narrative made the project lose its spark and he found it boring. He feels that the film version of *Something Wicked This Way Comes*, released in 1984, was a successful adaptation of the novel. Bradbury wrote the screenplay himself, and had a good sense of what elements of the book needed to be changed. His favorite film so far was 1998's *The Wonderful Ice Cream Suit*, about five men who pitch in to buy one suit to share. He wrote the screenplay for this one as well, and thought that the film came out beautifully. He was disappointed that it did not have a longer run in the theaters.

Warner Brothers Studio and actor/director Mel Gibson have been planning for a number of years on remaking *Fahrenheit 451*, but much to

Bradbury's disappointment, it keeps being delayed. Fortunately, another of his short stories, "A Sound of Thunder," was filmed in 2002. The time-travel story about how one butterfly can change the course of history is one of his most popular pieces.

Aside from writing for the big and small screens and writing fiction, Bradbury has a deep-seated love of the theater. After high school, he originally started writing plays until enough other writers whom he trusted urged him to stick to short stories. After *Fahrenheit 451* was published, Bradbury tried his hand at adapting it into a play. Unfortunately, it did not go over very well. He did not let that stop him, though, and over the years he has written and produced many plays with varying degrees of success.

> Bradbury felt that the film version of *Something Wicked This Way Comes* (1984), was a successful adaptation of his novel.

Bradbury's love of poetry led to the publication of his first collection in 1973. He has also written many articles and essays, one of which captured the attention of someone who would make one of Bradbury's longtime dreams—to design buildings at a World's Fair—come true. In 1963, he was given the job of designing part of the United States Pavilion for the 1964 World's Fair in New

York. As a child, he had gazed upon the futuristic buildings of the 1933 World's Fair, and now he would get to be a part of history. In addition to designing the attraction, he wrote a sixteen-minute film covering the history of the United States called *American Journey*. Twenty years later, he would be a part of another huge landmark in America's history. He was invited by his friend Walt Disney to help create a central attraction at Orlando's EPCOT center, called Spaceship Earth. He was very excited about this assignment, because unlike the World's Fair exhibit, EPCOT would be permanent.

Going to Orlando for the opening of EPCOT turned out to be a bigger personal milestone than he had imagined. After cancelled trains and car trouble on his journey from California, he agreed to fly home after the festivities. At sixty-three, this would be the first time he had ever been on an airplane. When he realized that he was not going to run up and down the aisles screaming—the fear that had kept him on the ground—he began to relax. He has now been all over the world, and has even flown on the Concord.[4]

After his work at EPCOT, he grew even more interested in designing the cities of the future, and in making them livable in the present. He was given that chance on a smaller scale, with the opportunity to help design local shopping plazas— the Glendale Galleria in Glendale, California, the Horton Plaza in San Diego, and the Westside Pavilion in Los Angeles. He set out to create places

Ray Bradbury designed Spaceship Earth in EPCOT Center. EPCOT stands for "Experimental Prototype Community of Tomorrow."

of beauty, where people could eat at outdoor cafés, and where they would feel safe and comfortable. According to Bradbury:

> If you can build a good museum, if you can make a good film, if you can build a good world's fair, if you can build a good mall, you're changing the future. You're influencing people, so that they'll get up in the morning and say, "Hey, it's worthwhile going to work." That's my function, and it should be the function of every science fiction writer around. To offer hope. To name the problem and then offer the solution. And I do, all the time. [5]

Chapter 8

A Living Legend

Bradbury was in London the night that Neil Armstrong and Buzz Aldrin landed on the moon in 1969. He left the studio of the talk show he was scheduled to be on, took a cab across town, and joined Mike Wallace and Walter Cronkite by satellite to share what the experience meant for him and for all of mankind. He was so moved by the knowledge that man had now walked on the moon that he wept. For the rest of the night he ran all over London appearing on nine other shows that were broadcast around the world. He talked about the meaning of life on such a momentous night:

We're always asking, "What are we doing here on earth?" We are the audience. There's no use having a universe, a cosmology, if you don't have witnesses. We are the witnesses to the miracle. We are put here by creation, by God, by the cosmos, whatever name you want to give it. We're here to be the audience to the magnificent. It is our job to celebrate.[2]

Thirty years later, Walter Cronkite gave him a tape of the show as a present. Bradbury had never seen it.[3]

In his eighties, Bradbury is as busy as ever. He continues to write every day, as he has for over sixty-eight years. In fact, he wrote part of a novel and an entire screenplay while hospitalized following a stroke in November 1999. For him, writing is a way of living forever, of following the advice that Mr. Electrico gave him when he was twelve. He believes that

[The inevitability of death] provokes you into creativity. That is the ricochet board that you work against. The sense of death has been with me always. It's a wall there and you bounce life off of it. And you create because there is the threat of extinction, so every new book is a triumph over darkness.[4]

Seeing no need for a computer, Bradbury still uses an electric typewriter. He delivers as many as a lecture a week at schools, libraries, writing conferences, and to audiences ranging from media executives to astronauts. Everywhere he speaks, he will sign books until the last person has left. He is a big supporter of libraries and speaks at branches all over the country, donating his time and the money from book sales. The funds all go

Walter Cronkite became famous as a television newscaster. He was the anchor of "The CBS Evening News" from 1962 to 1981.

back to the libraries so kids will have the same chance he did to fall in love with books. Bradbury loves encouraging young people to read and to express themselves through writing. For over twenty-five years, he has sponsored the Ray Bradbury Writing Contest through the Waukegan Public Library. He tells his audiences to read as much as they can, and to hold onto the things that excite them so that they will have something to write about. He implores them to enjoy life to the fullest, and not to watch local television news shows. "If you were to watch it every night, you'd think the world was coming to an end."[5]

Bradbury practices what he preaches. He finds joy in small things and likes to be surrounded by his treasures. He never throws anything away. His house is filled with antique rocket ships and ray guns, toy skeletons and submarines, a six-foot-tall Bullwinkle, robots, rubber monsters, ten magic sets, posters, and hundreds of trinkets and toys of all sorts. He keeps all his old typewriters because he believes there is magic in them.[6] His shelves are lined with nearly five thousand books. A big doodler, Bradbury paints as a hobby. He has always had an eye for art, and was very involved with the careers and visions of the artists who painted his book covers or illustrated his comic book adaptations.

Many children are familiar with Ray Bradbury because his books and short stories are often read in schools, especially *The Martian Chronicles* and *Fahrenheit 451*. Bradbury is one of the rare

Ray Bradbury's home office is filled with toys and treasures.

authors who is still beloved after they are "assigned reading." His explanation is:

> I deal in metaphors. All my stories are like the Greek and Roman myths, and the Egyptian myths, and the Old and New Testament. If you speak in tongues, if you write in metaphors, then people can remember them. The stories are very easy to recall, and you can tell them. So it's my ability as a teller of tales and a writer of metaphors. I think that's why I'm in the schools.[7]

A Bradbury scholar adds, "The trappings of science fiction may have attracted young people to Bradbury, but he has led them on to something much older and better: mythopoeic literature, normative truth acquired through wonder."[8] All together, there are now five installments of Bradbury's fictional autobiography: *Dandelion Wine* (1957), *Something Wicked This Way Comes* (1962), *Death is a Lonely Business* (1985), *A Graveyard for Lunatics* (1990), and *Green Shadows, White Whale* (1992). Much of his life experience and thoughts are reflected in these five books, hidden as fiction. Over his long career, he has also written book reviews, articles on outer space, politics, urban development, and creativity, plus many introductions to books on topics important to him.

Among the many awards bestowed upon him, Bradbury received the Medal for Distinguished Contribution to American Letters from the National Book Foundation on November 15, 2000. His other honors include the O. Henry Memorial Award, the Benjamin Franklin Award, the

World Fantasy Award for Lifetime Achievement, the Prometheus Award, the Jules Verne Award, The Bram Stoker Award, The Nebula Award, and the Grand Master Award from the Science Fiction Writers of America. He was inducted into the Science Fiction Hall of Fame in 1970.

Not many people can say they have a crater on the moon and a star here on Earth. In fact, Ray Bradbury is the only person alive who can claim such an honor. After landing on the moon in 1971, an Apollo astronaut named a crater

> "The trappings of science fiction may have attracted young people to Bradbury, but he has led them on to something much older and better: mythopoeic literature, normative truth acquired through wonder."
> —A Bradbury scholar

"Dandelion Crater," after Bradbury's book *Dandelion Wine*. Three decades later, Bradbury was given a star on Hollywood Boulevard to honor his achievements in film and broadcasting.

Bradbury hopes that in his lifetime NASA will put a man on Mars. Until then, he is going to keep writing every day, with no plans to retire. As he puts it, "God will have to hit me over the head with a baseball bat to get me off the plate."[9]

Peter Rowe, a journalist for the *San Diego Union-Tribune*, sums up Bradbury's legacy best: "Ray Bradbury's love of good writing and passion for life shine through his books. As great as his work is, perhaps the greatest thing he's written has been the script of his life."[10]

IN HIS OWN WORDS

On August 15, 2002, Ray Bradbury talked to me from his home in Los Angeles, California. With his eighty-second birthday only a week away, Bradbury still spoke with the fervor and excitement of youth.

Q: *Were you and your older brother, Skip, close growing up?*

A: I was the coward, the dreamer, the one afraid of everything. He was the athlete. He played football and surfed once we got out to California. He was one of the first surfers. At that time very few people surfed; you had to build your own surfboards. He didn't read books. I read them like crazy, and then I began writing when I was twelve, so we're totally different, and yet very affectionate.

Q: *Who were your role models when you were first starting out?*

A: Lon Chaney. I loved his films, like *Phantom of the Opera*. And Douglas Fairbanks, who I was named after—my middle name is Douglas. Then when I began to read extensively, Edgar Allen Poe, Jules Verne, H. G. Wells, and the various science fiction writers who were writing in the last part of the '20s, early '30s. I read Edgar Rice Burroughs—he was my superhero—and *Tarzan*. I wrote a sequel to one of

Burroughs's Martian books because he loved to leave his readers in suspense so you had to buy the next book in order to find our what happened next. I couldn't afford to buy the next book, so I wrote it.

Q: *Did you get it published?*

A: I was twelve! It was terrible. I threw it away.

Q: *What was your reaction when your first story was accepted for publication?*

A: I was twenty years old, and I lived at home with my parents and my brother. I sent a manuscript off to *Scripts*, which didn't pay anything, but it was a quality magazine—like the *New Yorker*—and a letter arrived at my home. I opened it down at the mailbox and I yelled for my mother and she ran down to see what was happening. She read the letter and we danced around the yard.

Q: *If you hadn't been a writer, what would you have done?*

A: I would have been a good librarian, a good bookseller, because I love books and libraries. I would have been a good teacher if I could have been patient. I don't know if I could've put up with the classroom, but on many levels, I would have liked to.

Q: *What would you say is different about the stories you write today compared to when you were younger?*

A: They are very much the same. Any idea that hits me, I write it. Some are very philosophical, some are poetic, some are crazy, some are humorous.

Q: *When you are working on a writing project, what is your daily schedule like?*

A: I usually have an idea very early in the morning or I wake up with an idea that occurs in my half sleep—when I'm not dreaming, but not quite awake. Then I jump out of bed and by noon I've finished a short story.

Q: *A few new movies based on your stories are slated to come out soon, and I know you've been disappointed with some of the results in the past. Are you looking forward to these new ones?*

A: I try not to think about it; it's gone on for so long. They've done seven drafts of *Fahrenheit 451* already. Some of the good news is at this very moment, in Prague [in the Czech Republic] they're filming my story "A Sound of Thunder," and wouldn't you know, God chose this moment to flood the place. I got a call from my production people that they're all stranded.

Q: *You give a lot of lot of talks at conferences, schools, and libraries. What do you enjoy about giving speeches?*

A: Well, I'm an actor. I acted on stage all during my school years, but I quit acting because I couldn't remember the lines—it drove me nuts. But then I learned I could have just as much fun by getting up and speaking, without notes, just having fun. So I love lecturing, because I am an actor. I can play the part and I have a good time.

Q: *Do you also enjoy reading your own books on tape for that reason?*

A: No, that's hard work. I get self-conscious. They turn out okay, but I don't enjoy it.

Q: *What was it like for you when the first Viking mission landed on Mars in 1976?*

A: It was wonderful. I was there with a few friends of mine at the Jet Propulsion Lab in Pasadena, California, along with various astronomers and rocket specialists . . . all celebrating, dancing around and laughing. At five in the morning an announcer from NBC asks me, "How does it feel, Mr. Bradbury, to have Viking land on Mars and there are no cities there, there are no people. You've been writing books your whole life about Mars." So I said, "Fool, fool, there are Martians on Mars and they are us. Look around; we are the Martians."

Q: *What would you say to a teenager who wants to be a writer?*

A: Fall in love with things. You've got to write about things you love. I loved Mars, and I loved Tarzan. There are a lot of books in the library, and they all say to just write. Write every day, and after about ten years or so, you become a writer.

Q: *How would you like to be remembered?*

A: As a person who loved what he was doing, and did it every day of his life. I feel very fortunate.

Timeline

1920—Ray Bradbury is born in Waukegan, Illinois, on August 22 to Leonard and Esther Bradbury.

1926—Younger sister, Elizabeth, is born. Family moves to Tucson, Arizona.

1927—Elizabeth passes away. Family returns to Waukegan.

1928—Ray first reads *Amazing Stories* and falls in love with science fiction and fantasy.

1932—Ray starts writing stories based on famous science fiction characters. Family moves back to Tucson. Ray gets a job reading comics over the radio.

1933—Family again moves back to Waukegan. Ray attends the World's Fair in Chicago.

1934—Family moves to Los Angeles.

1937—Ray joins the Los Angeles Science Fiction League.

1938—Ray graduates from Los Angeles High School.

1939—Publishes his own fanzine, *Futuria Fantasia*. Travels to New York to the first World Science Fiction Convention.

1941—Short story "Pendulum," co-authored with Henry Hasse, is published in *Super Science Stories*.

1943—First short stories written without outside assistance are published: "The Piper" in *Thrilling Wonder Stories*, and "The Wind" in *Weird Tales*.

1945—Short story, "The Black and White Game," is included in the *Best American Short Stories* anthology.

1947—Marries Marguerite (Maggie) McClure. Collection of short stories *Dark Carnival* is published. Don Congdon becomes his lifelong literary agent.

1948—Wins O. Henry Award for short story "Powerhouse."

1949—First daughter, Susan, is born. National Fantasy Fan Federation names him "Best Fantasy/Science Fiction Author of 1949."

1950—*The Martian Chronicles* is published. Family moves to West Los Angeles. *Dimension X* begins broadcasting.

1951—Second daughter, Ramona, is born. *The Illustrated Man* is published.

1952—Writes idea for film, *It Came from Outer Space*.

1953—Novel *Fahrenheit 451* and short story collection *Golden Apples of the Sun* are published. Family moves to Ireland for seven months so Bradbury can write the screenplay to *Moby Dick*. *Time* calls him "The Poet of the Pulps."

1955—Third daughter, Bettina, is born. Short story collection *The October Country* and children's book *Switch on the Night* are published.

1957—Father passes away. *Dandelion Wine* is published.

1958—Fourth daughter, Alexandra, is born.

1959—Short story collection, *A Medicine for Melancholy*, is published.

1962—Novel, *Something Wicked This Way Comes*, and short story collection for teenagers, *R Is for Rocket*, are published.

1963—Nominated for Academy Award for animated short film, *Icarus Montgolfier Wright*. Publishes first collection of drama, *The Anthem Sprinters and Other Antics*.

1964—Works on American exhibit at New York's World's Fair. Short story collection *Machineries of Joy* is published.

1965—Short story "The Other Foot" is selected to be in *Fifty Best American Short Stories: 1915–1965*.

1966—Mother passes away. The film version of *Fahrenheit 451* directed by François Truffaut is released.

1969—The film version of *The Illustrated Man* is released. Short story collection, *I Sing the Body Electric!*, is published.

1970—The Science Fiction Writers of America selects short story "Mars Is Heaven!" for the Science Fiction Hall of Fame.

1972—Children's book, *The Halloween Tree*, is published.

1973—First poetry collection, *When Elephants Last in the Dooryard Bloomed*, is published.

1977—Receives a Lifetime Achievement Award at the World Fantasy Convention.

1980—Short story collection, *The Stories of Ray Bradbury,* is published. Receives Grandmaster of Fantasy Gandalf Award at the Hugo Award Ceremonies. *The Martian Chronicles* television miniseries airs.

1984—Film version of *Something Wicked This Way Comes* is released. Receives the Jules Verne Award.

1985—Novel, *Death Is a Lonely Business*, is published.

1988—Receives Grand Master Nebula Award by The Science Fiction and Fantasy Writers of America.

1989—Receives Bram Stoker Award for Lifetime Achievement by the Horror Writers Association.

1990—Novel, *A Graveyard for Lunatics*, and book of essays, *Zen in the Art of Writing*, are published.

1992—Novel about Ireland, *Green Shadows, White Whale*, is published.

1994—*The Halloween Tree* wins Emmy Award for Best Animated Children's Program.

1996—*Quicker than the Eye* is published.

1997—Story collection, *Driving Blind*, is published.

2000—Receives the Medal for Distinguished Contribution to American Letters from the National Book Foundation.

2001—Novel in stories, *From the Dust Returned*, is published fifty-five years after Bradbury first started working on it.

2002—Given a star on Hollywood Boulevard. Story collection, *One More for the Road*, is published.
Let's All Kill Constance is published.

2003—Marguerite Bradbury passes away.

2004—*The Cat's Pajamas: New Stories* is published.

Selected Works

1947—*Dark Carnival*
1950—*The Martian Chronicles*
1951—*The Illustrated Man*
1953—*Fahrenheit 451*
    The Golden Apples of the Sun
1957—*Dandelion Wine*
1962—*Something Wicked This Way Comes*
    R Is for Rocket
1963—*The Anthem Sprinters and Other Antics*
1964—*Machineries of Joy*
1966—*S Is for Space*
1972—*The Halloween Tree*
    The Wonderful Ice Cream Suit and Other Plays
1976—*Long After Midnight*
1985—*Death Is a Lonely Business*
1990—*Zen in the Art of Writing*
    A Graveyard for Lunatics
1991—*Yestermorrow: Obvious Answers to Impossible Futures*
1992—*Green Shadows, White Whale*
1996—*Quicker than the Eye*
1997—*Driving Blind*
    Dogs Think That Every Day Is Christmas

Selected Works

With Cat for Comforter
Driving Blind
1998—*Ahmed and the Oblivion Machines*
I Sing the Body Electric! and Other Stories
2001—*From the Dust Returned*
They Have Not Seen the Stars
2002—*One More for the Road*
Let's All Kill Constance
2004—*The Cat's Pajamas: New Stories*

Words to Know

allusion—In literature, an implied reference.

anthology—A collection of stories by different authors.

collaboration—When two or more people work together on a project.

evokes—Brings to mind or recreates imaginatively.

genre—A category of literature.

Great Depression—A period of high unemployment and low business activity that occurred in the 1930s.

idealize—To make something grander that it actually is.

macabre—Gruesome; having to do with death.

metaphor—A figure of speech in which a word or phrase is used as a symbol in place of another to suggest a likeness or analogy.

paean—Expression of joy or praise: a written, spoken, or musical expression of enthusiastic praise or rapturous joy.

ravine—A small, narrow valley that usually is marked by running water.

simile—A figure of speech comparing two unlike things that is often introduced with the words "like" or "as."

speculative—Relating to an intellectual assumption; based on theory.

subvert—To corrupt or overthrow.

unrequited—Not reciprocated or returned.

theme—A central subject or idea.

transition—A movement or passage from one subject to another.

CHAPTER NOTES

Preface

1. Ray Bradbury, "Drunk, and in Charge of a Bicycle," introduction to *The Stories of Ray Bradbury* (New York: Alfred A. Knopf, 1980), p. xiii.
2. Ray Bradbury, "The Eyrie," *Weird Tales*, November 1943, pp. 109–110.
3. Mary Roach, "Questions for Ray Bradbury, Martian Tourist," *New York Times Magazine*, November 2000, Section 6, p. 21.
4. Frederik Pohl, ed., *The SFWA Grand Masters: Volume Two* (New York: Tom Doherty Associates, 2000), pp. 396–397.
5. Wayne L. Johnson, "The Invasion Stories of Ray Bradbury," *Ray Bradbury: Modern Critical Views*, edited by Harold Bloom (Philadelphia: Chelsea House, 2001), p. 22.
6. Ray Bradbury, *The October Country* (New York: Ballantine, 1955), p iii.
7. David Mogen, *Ray Bradbury* (Boston: Twayne, 1986), p. 13.
8. Robin Anne Reid, *Ray Bradbury: A Critical Companion* (Westport, Conn.: Greenwood Press, 2000), p. 14.
9. William R. Nolan, *The Ray Bradbury Companion* (Detroit: Gale Research, 1975), p. 5.

Chapter 1. Meeting the Magicians

1. Thomas M. Sipos, "Ray Bradbury on Mel Gibson's *Fahrenheit 451*, preaching science, and the universe," April 22, 2002, <http://www. hollywoodinvestigator.com/ 2002/bradbury.htm> (December 1, 2002).

2. Dorian Benkoil, "Ray Bradbury writes for 'Love'," *Associated Press*, December 6, 1996.

3. Harry Blackstone, *The Blackstone Book of Magic & Illusion* (New York: Newmarket Press, 985), p. viii.

4. Ray Bradbury, "Happy Birthday to me!" *In His Words*, August 29, 2002, <http://www.raybradbury. com/inhiswords.html> (December 1, 2002).

5. Ibid.

6. Ray Bradbury, *Dandelion Wine* (New York: Doubleday, 1957), pp. 9–11.

Chapter 2. The Wonder Years

1. Jared Dunn, "Art," n.d., <http://www. suspensionofdisbelief.org/think/q-art.txt> (March 14, 2004).

2. Ben P. Indick, "Ray Bradbury: Still talking and still listening," *Publishers Weekly*, New York, Oct. 22, 2001, p. 40.

3. Daneet Steffens, "Ray Bradbury's Ghosts," *Book Magazine*, September/October 2001.

4. David Mogen, *Ray Bradbury* (Boston: Twayne, 1986), p. 2.

5. John Flink, "Ray Bradbury Comes Home," *The Chicago Tribune*, November 17, 1996, p. 5.

6. Robert R. Rees, "Ray Bradbury—Emissary or Missionary," *Magical Blend Magazine*, Issue #51, April 1996.

Chapter 3. Hooray for Hollywood

1. David Mogen, *Ray Bradbury* (Boston: Twayne, 1986), pp. 5–6.
2. As quoted in Katie de Koster, ed., *Readings on Fahrenheit 451* (San Diego: CA: Greenhaven Press, 2000), p. 18.
3. Jerry Weist, *Bradbury: An Illustrated Life* (New York: William Morrow, 2002), pp. 12–13.
4. Shel Horowitz, "Ray Bradbury's Wild Dreams Become Reality: Bradbury Speaks at the University of Massachusetts/Amherst," *Global Arts Review*, n.d., <http://www.frugalfun.com/review.html> (December 1, 2002).
5. Ibid.
6. Wiest, pp. 10, 18.
7. Ray Bradbury, "Drunk, and in Charge of a Bicycle," introduction to *The Stories of Ray Bradbury* (New York: Alfred A. Knopf, 1980), p. xviii.

Chapter 4. Bradbury's Early Career and Marriage

1. Christopher Isherwood, *Tomorrow*, October 1950, pp. 56–58.
2. Ray Bradbury, "Interview," *Future*, October 1978.
3. *Ray Bradbury: An American Icon*. Monterey Home Video, Great North Productions, Inc. 1997.
4. Wayne L. Johnson, *Ray Bradbury* (New York: Frederick Ungar Publishing Co., 1980), pp. 4–5.
5. Ray Bradbury, "The Fog Horn," *The Vintage Bradbury* (New York: Vintage Books, 1965), p. 268.
6. Johnson, pp. 5–9.

Chapter 5. The Martian Chronicles

1. Russell Kirk, "The World of Ray Bradbury," *Enemies of the Permanent Things* (New Rochelle, N.Y.: Arlington House, 1969), pp. 120, 124.

2. Ray Bradbury, *Introduction to The Martian Chronicles* (New York: Avon, 1997), p. viii.
3. Sam Weller, "Semper Sci-Fi: As he Turns 80, Waukegan Favorite Son Ray Bradbury Stays Ever Faithful to his Fantastical Style," *Chicago Tribune*, August 13, 2000, p. 10.
4. A. James Stupple, "Ray Bradbury," *Voices for the Future: Essays on Major Science Fiction Writers, Vol. 1*, ed. Thomas D. Clareson (Ohio: Bowling Green University Popular Press, 1976), p. 177.
5. Robert Kanigel, *Vintage Reading* (Baltimore, Md.: Bancroft Press, 1998), p. 165.
6. Joshua Klein, "Interview with Ray Bradbury," *The Onion A.V. Club*, Vol. 35, issue 23, June 17, 1999.

Chapter 6. Fahrenheit 451

1. Katie de Koster, ed., *Readings on Fahrenheit 451* (San Diego: CA: Greenhaven Press, 2000), pp. 15–16.
2. *Ray Bradbury: An American Icon*. Monterey Home Video, Great North Productions, Inc. 1997.
3. Scott Eyman, "Q&A with Ray Bradbury," *Palm Beach Post*, Sunday, March 10, 2002.
4. George R. Guffey, "*Fahrenheit 451* and the 'Cubby-Hole Editors' of Ballantine Books," *Coordinates: Placing Science Fiction and Fantasy*, ed. George E. Slusser, Eric S. Rabkin, and Robert Scholes (Illinois: Southern Illinois University Press, 1983), pp. 99–106.
5. Ray Bradbury, *Fahrenheit 451* (New York: Ballantine, 1953), p. 54.
6. Ray Bradbury, quoted in *The Independent*, London, July 16, 1992.

Chapter 7. Books and Beyond

1. Marshall Berges, "Bradbury Hears Voices in the Night," *The Los Angeles Times*, April 17, 1985, p. 1.
2. Harold Bloom, ed., *Modern Fantasy Writers* (New York: Chelsea House, 1995), p. 2.
3. Katie de Koster, ed., *Readings on Fahrenheit 451* (San Diego: Calif.: Greenhaven Press, 2000), pp. 25–26.
4. J. Stephen Bolhafner, "The Ray Bradbury Chronicles," *The St. Louis Post-Dispatch*, December 1, 1996, p. 3C.
5. Robert Couteau, "A Romance of Places: An Interview with Ray Bradbury," *Quantum: Science Fiction & Fantasy Review*, Spring 1991, p. 39.

Chapter 8. A Living Legend

1. Joshua Klein, "Interview with Ray Bradbury," *The Onion A.V. Club*, Vol 35, issue 23, June 17, 1999.
2. Ray Bradbury, *Ray Bradbury's Award Speech* at National Book Awards Ceremony, New York, N.Y., November 15, 2000, <http://www.raybradbury.com/awards_acceptance.html> (March 12, 2004).
3. Robin Miller, "Ray Bradbury: Following his Passion to Mars," *The Town Talk*, February 2000. <http://www.raybradbury.com/articles_town_talk.html> (December 1, 2002).
4. Sandy Hill, "Science Fiction Supernova," *The Charlotte Observer*, October 12, 1997, p. 1F.
5. Miller.
6. Ray Bradbury, "Bringing dreams to reality," *R & D*, September 28, 1992, p. 14.
7. Klein.

8. Russell Kirk, "The World of Ray Bradbury," *Enemies of the Permanent Things* (New Rochelle, N.Y.: Arlington House, 1969), p. 124.

9. Bob Minzesheimer, "Bradbury still burns with literary light," *USA Today*, November 18, 2000.

10. Joseph Cervantes, *Ray Bradbury Headlines at Sixth Annual Writer's Symposium by the Sea*, February 27, 2001, <http://www.ptloma.edu/viewpoint/Sp01/WritersSym.htm> (December 1, 2002).

FURTHER READING

Books

Bradbury, Ray. *Zen in the Art of Writing*. New York: Bantam Books, 1992.

Bradbury, Ray. *The Vintage Bradbury*. New York: Vintage Books, 1965.

de Koster, Katie, ed. *Readings on Fahrenheit 451*. San Diego: CA: Greenhaven Press, 2000.

Johnson, Wayne L. *Ray Bradbury*. New York: Frederick Ungar Publishing Co., 1980.

Mogen, David. *Ray Bradbury*. Boston: Twayne, 1986.

Nolan, William F. *The Ray Bradbury Companion*. Detroit: Gale Research, 1975.

Reid, Robin Anne. *Ray Bradbury: A Critical Companion*. Westport, CT: Greenwood Press, 2000.

Wiest, Jerry. *Bradbury: An Illustrated Life*. New York: William Morrow, 2002.

Video

Ray Bradbury: An American Icon. Monterey Home Video, Great North Productions, Inc. 1997.

INTERNET Addresses

Author Profile: Ray Bradbury
http://www.teenreads.com/authors/
au-bradbury-ray.asp

Official Ray Bradbury Site
http://www.raybradbury.com

Ray Bradbury Online
http://www.spaceagecity.com/bradbury/
index.htm

Index